ISBN 9798340153951
First Edition
Journey Life Balance Inc.
jennifer@journeylifebalance.com
www.journeylifebalance.com

A booklet for caregivers, family and friends

WHO AM I NOW?

Jennifer L. Rowe, LCSW

The article "Who Am I Now? The Ever-changing Role of the Caregiver" was based on years of assisting a friend, Toni, who worked at the local Office for the Aging. She would host a caregiver series and ask me to talk about an aspect of caregiving.

When you have friends in your field who are connected to your work, you get recruited to do things with them. My memory of the conversations involves Toni telling me I would present as part of her caregiver series and me saying, "No. I don't want to. I am too busy." I recall Toni saying something like, "Yes, you have to." I also remember her offering incentives, including me being able to leave my job early to meet her and have lunch at nearby restaurants.

I developed a presentation that turned into an article and later I published it. As I was creating this program, I started to weave in stories of caregivers I had worked with and my own. I think narratives are important ways to connect and communicate.

All stories written in this publication have been combined with multiple individuals, are intentionally modified, and relationships are deliberately altered to create additional privacy. Any similarities to the content are purely coincidental. AI was not used to generate any of the content in this booklet.

Professional and personal stories will be used, as well as humor, to bring home points of specific caregiver situations and identify role changes. I utilize a social work perspective as this is the field I work in.

With gratitude,
Jennifer L. Rowe, LCSW
Owner of Journey Life Balance Inc
Social Worker with over 30 years of experience

CHAPTER 1
05
Caregivers
Caregiver Experiences
Caregiver Role Changes

CHAPTER 2
10
Family
Family Meeting
Family Member Strengths

CHAPTER 3
12
Roles
Family Roles
Job Titles and Adaptation

CHAPTER 4
17
What If
What If... Questions and Service Options

CHAPTER 5
22
Caregiver
Physical Needs and Self-Care
Crisis Prevention and Services
Perceptions and Emotions

CHAPTER 6
28
Support
Respite Service Options
Financial Aspects
Support Systems

CHAPTER 7
32
How Social Workers & Healthcare Professionals Can Help

34
Resources

TABLE OF CONTENTS

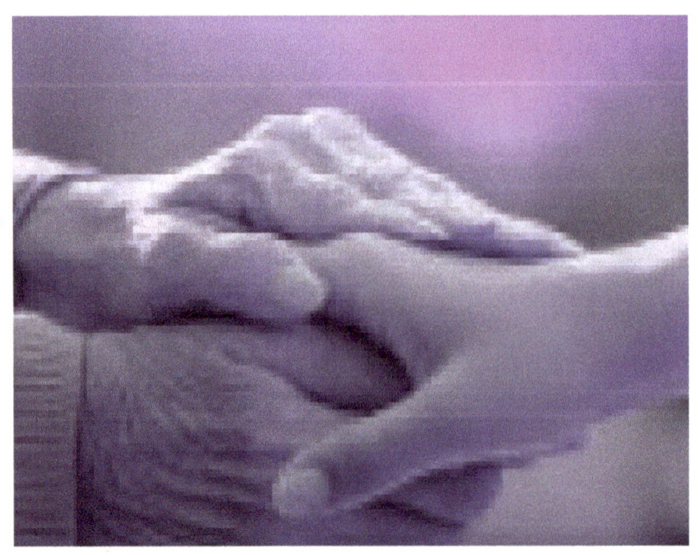

Daughter of Joan and John

Sibling of Lori and Kristen

Mother of Johnathan and Jason

Lover and partner of Mike

Cat owner of Echo, Flash, Louie, and Wonder Woman

Dog owner of Benny

Inheritor of matriarchal autoimmune genes

Social worker of 30 years

Owner of Journey Life Balance Inc

Writer/Educator

Adventure seeker

Lifelong learner

Throughout this publication, you will see me use the term caregivers. I recognize terminology changes, but I honor the vocabulary or word choices of the clients I work with, and the majority have identified themselves to me as a caregiver.

I also use the concept of space and a nebula throughout this book as I think of personal growth as limitless, and at times, what may come next is unknown. I like not knowing who we are, as life can change.

"

I want to thank my friend, Toni N., the Ethel to my Lucy, who asked me to create a presentation many years ago, and it became so much more.

I want to thank the caregivers, clients, patients, interdisciplinary team members, friends, and others I have worked with personally and professionally.

CHAPTER ONE

CAREGIVER EXPERIENCES

I have worked with caregivers who feel they cannot ask for assistance…
Those who neglect their health to care for a loved one…
Who expect to provide excellent care…
And those judged by family or friends when expressing emotion or stress!
I have had caregivers cry when I have asked them how they are feeling
or managing and whisper, "No one ever asks me that."
I have heard expressions of guilt, especially when I worked for the
Alzheimer's Association and then transitioned into an area nursing home
that had an Alzheimer's care unit. I had clients for years between both
work environments. The expressions of guilt I often heard were:

- "Mom said she never wanted to go into a nursing home."

- "I promised Dad I would always care for him at home."

- "I did not know how much a support group would help me feel less alone."

CAREGIVER ROLE CHANGES

Role changes depend on the household dynamic...
- The caregiver who has never managed money
  may now be managing finances.
- The caregiver who never cooked is now the
  one cooking.

PERSONAL STORY

My former in-laws struggled with physical and mental conditions. Physically, my mother-in-law was disabled and used a wheelchair. Mentally, she was alert, oriented, and capable. My father-in-law was mentally fading due to dementia but physically able to do everything. They balanced each other until his health declined, he passed, and six months later, she passed. Before their decline, there were multiple family conversations about what to do **WHEN** something happened, not **IF** something happened. The first complication was my in-laws were living in Florida.

- The nearest family lived in California, New York, Ohio, Pennsylvania, and Virginia.
- Their children could not agree on what to do, which created conflict and brought out long-standing sibling dynamics, which we often witness as social workers.
- There were legal issues due to disagreement between their financial Power of Attorney and their Healthcare Proxy agent. *(Author note: These titles/terms vary by state. In this situation, one family member oversaw monetary affairs, and the other oversaw healthcare decision-making).*
- One sibling had no interest in providing physical or financial care for her parents, although the two male siblings expected her to provide care as the daughter.
- When my father-in-law passed, the two sons swooped in and moved mom. She was moved out of state and placed in an apartment near other family members. Family members stopped by to bring her meals and set up her medications in a pill box. She began wandering out of her apartment and getting lost in the town as she was unfamiliar with the area. She began to under and then overtake her medications as she would forget she had taken them.
- As a social worker, I was frustrated as I had a strong healthcare background and worked in geriatrics at the time. The family would not listen to my suggestions regarding resources and service options.

SUMMARY OF SERVICE OPTIONS

The family could have considered several options.

My mother-in-law could have remained in Florida with the following services in place:

a. Home-delivered meals – such as Meals on Wheels or Mom's Meals.

b. A Companion Service – is a program where a non-medical caregiver enters the home for companionship, light housekeeping, medication reminders, and meal preparation. Some programs offer transportation. Some do not. Companion care is usually not covered by insurance and is paid privately.

c. An aide could have been hired to maintain her in her home if she needed medical care.

d. Life alert (A 24-hour emergency call device could have been installed in the home) or another alerting system could have been used. Some smartphones have fall detection options. This option is usually a feature paired with a smartwatch. You have to use the health app or download an app.

e. She could have been enrolled in a pharmacy pre-packaged medication program:
    - Medications are prepackaged in blister packs.
    - Packs are labeled by morning, afternoon, evening, and bedtime to help manage medication dosing and reduce medication errors, as there are no longer multiple pill bottles to manage.
    - A local or mail-order pharmacy delivers medications.

f. A neighbor, family friend, or church member may have assisted with errand running, grocery shopping, preparing meals, and transportation to appointments.

g. Some towns have low-cost senior transportation programs. There is an application to complete for the service, and it can take a few weeks to process the paperwork and set up the transportation. This may have been an option for getting her to and from medical appointments.

h. Local agencies – could have been contacted, including the social service agency in her county. A search for a local area agency on aging may have helped provide referrals to area resources. A geriatric care/case manager, or agencies that assist seniors could have been found. Some local agencies have volunteers who help seniors.

After she was moved, the family could have considered the above and the following options:

a. Senior housing instead of an apartment with no supervision. She could have had companions, an aide, and the services listed above utilized in her new town.

b. Family members worked during the day, and my mother-in-law could have been enrolled in an adult day care program for socialization and meals.

c. Cameras could have been installed inside and outside the home to monitor her during the day and reduce the risk of wandering.

Role Change with Community Resources
(Assumptions and Expectations)

I have seen a variety of situations related to this:

- Loved ones may reject or be hostile to aides, especially in cases where someone has dementia.

> I worked with a daughter whose mother had Alzheimer's,
> and the mother kept firing the aides the daughter hired.
> She was threatening the aides with her cane and kept
> telling them, "You need to get out of my home."

- I have seen families struggle with seeking resources, including my own family.

PERSONAL STORY

My mother has Multiple Sclerosis and, at the time, used a walker as her means of mobility. My parents decided to move my paternal grandmother into their home. My grandmother had Parkinson's and used a walker. She was not able to bathe or dress herself. My father believed my mother could bathe and dress my grandmother. He did not want "strangers" in the home, wanted to dictate the hours for an aide as he wanted an aide at 10:00 a.m., and truly believed my mother would be my grandmother's caregiver while he worked.

My sisters and I met to discuss the situation and strategize options. We had a pre-meeting before the family meeting with our parents. We met with my parents to address our concerns. We focused on safety, the need for my grandmother to have an aide for her care needs, and the areas of limitations within my father's plan. Fortunately, I have a sister who is a physical therapist who explained the physical aspects of bathing and dressing someone and how my mother could not do this while using her walker in a shared showering space. I brought in my strengths as a social worker. I explained to my father that agencies have a schedule for their aides as the aides often have multiple clients per day. I also shared the limitations of health insurance as an aide is not covered for long-term care needs and called agencies that staffed my parents' town as they are in a town with limited aide service options. In our situation, we were fortunate to find an agency with an aide my family knew! Growing up, my sister and I played sports against her daughter!

SUMMARY OF SERVICE OPTIONS

a. We set up a family meeting – my sisters and I met with my parents.

b. We identified our parents' concerns.

c. We educated our parents about caregiving concerns – bathing, dressing, community services, and insurance.

d. We called home care agencies to see who could assist. The agency sent a nurse to the home to evaluate my grandmother and approve a certain number of hours for care each week.

e. We found an aide perfect for my grandmother, and they developed a strong bond.

CHAPTER TWO

FAMILY MEETING

When I worked for the Alzheimer's Association, I would go into the community and clients' homes to facilitate family meetings. The advice I give to caregivers is to think of the family in the context of a sports team:

- Who is the strongest player on the team? Is there a sibling/child/friend that mom or dad listens to over all the others, possibly someone they respect and value the opinion of?
- Who is the weakest link?
    - ◆ I once mediated a family pre-meeting before seeing a man needing assistance. I asked his children who the weakest link was, the person most likely to give into Dad's desire to remain unsafe in the home (he had set several kitchen fires, had hit cars in parking lots and the house with his car), and four of the siblings pointed to one specific sibling. Dad would go to her when he did not like something and align with her. She would give in to what Dad wanted to not upset him, which would cause conflict with her siblings, who were worried about his safety. During the pre-meeting, the siblings turned to the one sister and pointed at her as we met. They expressed frustration with the meeting, creating a plan, their sister agreeing with the plan and then changing her mind to agree with their father. I worked on coaching her and told her I wanted her to have a script or mantra she would say to her Dad if this happened after the family meeting. We rehearsed options such as, "Dad, we all agree this is the best option." and "I agree with the family."

During a family meeting, it is important to work closely with the family members on boundaries and look at the individuality of each caregiver, the loved one's overall needs, and areas where the loved one could reasonably maintain independence. I define reasonably maintained independence when considering safety concerns related to supervision, fall risk, fire setting, unsafe driving, and not taking medication as prescribed. Safety is always a priority.

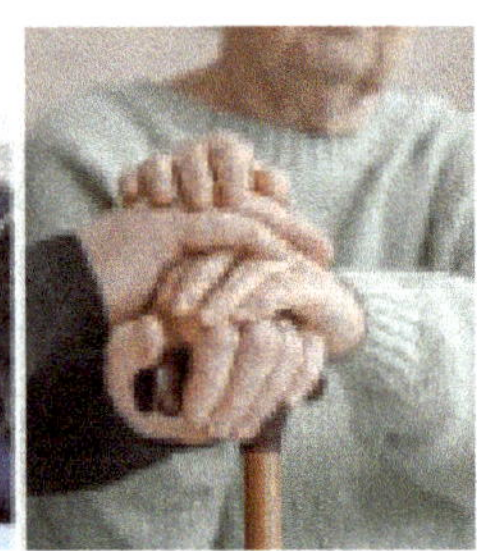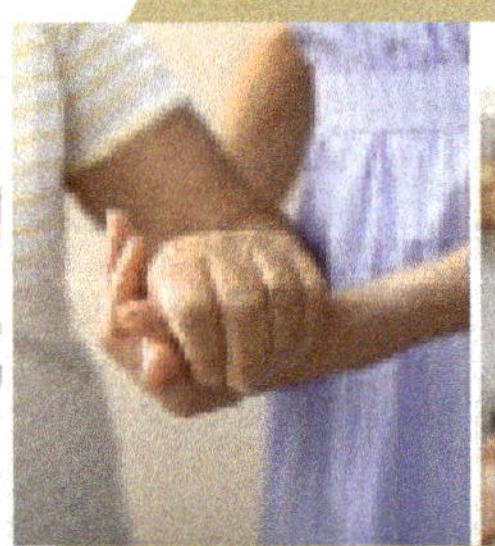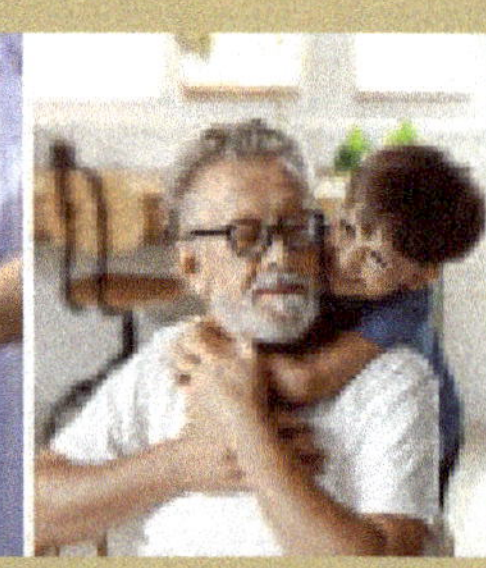

FAMILY MEMBER STRENGTHS

I also want you to consider the strengths of those who may assist. Here are a few examples of roles for family members.

Is there:
- A natural financial planner? Is someone good at managing money or putting the bills online to pay them on behalf of a loved one?
- A person who will take over the medical coordination (in my family, this is my middle sister, as she is a physical therapist in a rehabilitation hospital and works with a large health-care team). My sister takes over the medical coordination, contacts doctors and discharge planners during hospitalizations of loved ones, and joins in interdisciplinary meetings. She is also able to identify equipment or resources needed for physical care.
- A person who can make phone calls. This can be a way for long-distance family members to assist by finding agencies or conducting internet searches for resources. (My sister in Massachusetts and I often split this role).
- A tech-savvy person can set up doorbell cameras or devices to monitor safety.
- Can an organizer set up pill boxes, organize mail, and label cabinets or food items?
- Can a person who enjoys cooking prepare extra meals they freeze and give to the caregiver who can defrost and reheat them?
- Can a person pay for a meal delivery service?
- Who will take care of any pets in the home?

Recognize family members who may not want to have a caregiving role. Some family members do not want to be caregivers, may have had a complicated relationship within the family context, or there is a family dynamic or history, and some cannot be caregivers due to their life circumstances.

SUMMARY OF ROLES

•Cook	•Financial Planner	•Housekeeper
•Meal Service Payor	•Medical Coordinator	•Money Manager
•Organizer	•Pet Care Coordinator	•Phone Call Maker
	•Tech Support	

CHAPTER THREE

CONSIDER INTER-GENERATIONAL ROLES

- In marriages with traditional gender roles, a wife may expect or be expected to be the caregiver.
- Has the wife/mother always managed the home and cared for the family unit?
- What if the wife/mother gets sick… a husband/father in a family with a similar dynamic may expect his daughters to care for their mother.

Adult Children/Grandchildren
- May expect equal roles for siblings to share in caregiving. In some family situations, this may not be possible due to events in their siblings' lives or distance.
- May feel guilty for not being comfortable with aspects of care such as physical care.
    - I worked with a son who was an only child, and his mother had Alzheimer's. She had lost bladder and bowel control. She was not able to bathe herself. He was not comfortable bathing his mother or changing her adult incontinence supplies (Depends).
- May be caught between raising their own family and the needs of a loved one.
- An adult granddaughter may take on the caregiving of grandparents.
    - I worked with one granddaughter who lived next door to her grandparents. She was a stay-at-home mom of a newborn, who was assisting her grandparents by making meals and transporting them to their appointments. She loved seeing her grandparents daily, and they loved spending time with her newborn.

What If There Is No Family to Help?

I would look to see who the person may have connections with within the community.
Are they part of a church or group? Are there friends or a neighbor who can step in? Some agencies can assist. I recommend the local area agency on aging and the Department of
Social Services, as well as contacting local agencies and speaking to primary care physicians
during doctor visits. If a person is hospitalized, social workers and nurse case managers are great
resources for information.

Exploitation

I wish I could say I have never encountered ill-intentioned family members, neighbors,
or other predators but unfortunately, I have. I strongly recommend contacting Adult
Protective Services (this name may vary by state, but it is usually a part of the Department
of Social Services), local law enforcement, and some counties have elder task forces. I have seen
the physical, emotional, mental, and financial exploitation of elders. As a mandated
reporter, I have made multiple reports to these agencies during my career. The challenge
of adult services is that there are limitations as adults can choose to stay in the situation.

- Early in my career, I worked for Adult Protective Services. I worked with an elderly
  gentleman whom a teen grandson physically abused. The grandson had pointed a gun
  at his grandfather and pistol-whipped him to the point of bruising, stitches, and need for
  hospitalization for a concussion. The grandfather chose to stay in the situation and said
  to me, "I know he (grandson) will probably kill me someday, but I am the only family he
  has." The grandfather was alert and oriented to all spheres per a psychiatric evaluation
  and could choose to keep the grandson in the home. After several incidents, the police
  were able to press charges against the grandson and place him in a juvenile program for
  offenders. The grandson was removed from the grandfather's home.

HEALTH ADVOCATE

Health advocate - the person who interfaces with hospitals, doctors, home care agencies, etc.

Insurance interpreter - insurance is complex. This person may read the insurance Explanation of Benefits (EOB), check the policy for what is and is not covered by the insurance, monitor deductibles, and explore options for in and out-of-network benefits.

Medical terminology translator – this can be a challenge if the person does not understand medical terminology. They may not understand what the doctor is saying. Social workers and other healthcare professionals are skilled at translating. They can explain advance directives such as a full code, living will, healthcare proxy, and do not resuscitate. They are proficient in terminology related to insurance and medical care.

- I had a dialysis patient whose wife was ill with COVID. His wife was hospitalized, and the client was not allowed the visit due to COVID-19 hospital restrictions. I checked on the client each week to ask about his wife. The client began to tell me his wife was intubated (artificially being given air via a tube) and brain dead, but the doctors told him his wife had to get through the next 48 hours. The doctors had asked him about artificial nutrition (tube feeding). I was confused by what the client was telling me as he was hopeful about the next 48 hours and thought his wife would recover. He then shared that the hospital asked him to make his wife a Do Not Resuscitate (DNR). One of my nephrologists was rounding in the clinic, and I pulled him aside to explain that something did not seem right with what the client was sharing. His nephrologist and I met with the client after his dialysis treatment, and the nephrologist explained the medical terminology to the client in a way the client understood. The client asked his nephrologist to call his wife's doctor with the client present and clarify what he was told. The client was stunned when his wife's doctor explained his wife was not doing well and if she survived the next 48 hours, she would be on life support as she had no brain function and would never eat or breathe on her own.

Years ago, my mother was hospitalized and given the wrong medication post-surgery. She was not alert, awake, or verbally responsive and was transferred to a local rehabilitation hospital. My father and sister are her healthcare agents and can legally make medical decisions. When the surgical hospital sent her to the rehab hospital, her advance directive paperwork did not transfer with her. The nurse was admitting my mother to the rehab and asking my father and I questions. The nurse asked my dad if my mom was a Full Code or Do Not Resuscitate (DNR). My father told the nurse my mother was a DNR. My mother **WAS NOT A DNR**, but because I was not listed as a decision maker and could not reach my sister on the phone, the hospital was going to list my mother as a DNR, as the prior hospital's records noted my dad as the decision maker. I was pleading with the hospital not to make my mom a DNR.

Frustrated, I asked my Dad, "Do you know what a DNR is?"

Dad said, "No."

I replied, "It means Mom is Dead, Not Returning." (This is a term I like to use with non-medical professionals to understand the term, "do not resuscitate.")

My Dad said, "That's not what your Mom is. She wants everything done."

My Dad did not understand the terminology. When my Mom woke up, she modified her advanced directives and made my sister and other family members her decision-makers. As a family, we realized there needed to be someone with more medical knowledge who could talk with the hospital.

CAREGIVER ADAPTATION TO ROLE CHANGES

- A person who never food shopped or cooked is now managing these tasks.
- A person who has never managed family finances is balancing a checkbook or budgeting.
- Role reversal is common between parents and their children and is often common for individuals with cognitive impairments. Reversals can be a challenge as the assistance offered may not be welcomed.

  - ◆ A son I worked with hired an aide for his mother, and his mother would lock the door to not let the aide into the home. The son would leave the door unlocked for the aide to enter the home, and his mother would lock it once he left. We troubleshooted options, including leaving a key hidden for the aide. His mother then responded by calling the police on the aide to say there were strangers in her home or someone had broken in. Sometimes, she would call 911, yell "help," and hang up. The police would arrive at the door. The son and I had a second meeting and devised another plan. We had the aide text him when she arrived, and he would call his mother on her house phone to say there would be a woman in the home who was there to help him and ensure mom ate. His mother would let the aide into the home if she had spoken with her son.

- There are times a person may choose to give up independence, such as someone recognizing they are not driving safely. Other times, a family member must take away the keys, or doctors can send letters/forms to revoke driver's licenses. In some states, DMV mandates vision tests after a certain age. Some states offer physical driving safety courses.
- A person needing care may minimize their needs so as not to burden their family. As a social worker, I try remembering this when meeting with a loved one or caregiver. I look at what the person in need of care wants. What is their goal? Is it independence? To not be a burden? To remain in their home?
- Someone may have to assist with pet care or placing pets in a new home.

CHAPTER FOUR

WHAT IF... QUESTIONS

At the forefront of consciousness is the **WHAT IF**....

These are the four in-the-morning questions that wake us with worry.

- **What if** mom/dad falls in the middle of the night?

- **What if** dad takes the car and has another accident?

- **What if** mom needs more care than I can provide?

WHAT IFs begin when a loved one's physical or personal safety changes.

WHAT IF... SERVICE OPTIONS

- Adult Day Programs
- Companion Services
- Home-Delivered Meals
- Hospice
- Pet Caretaker

- Assisted Living
- Continuing Care Communities
- Home Health Care
- Nursing Home (Skilled Nursing Facility)
- Senior Housing

The above services can be used individually or in conjunction.

ADULT DAY PROGRAMS

There are two types of adult daycare programs: the medical and social models. The medical model involves more intensive health care (a nurse manages medications while in the program), and there may be therapy services (physical, occupational, and speech therapy). Physical care for Activities of Daily Living is provided; physical toileting, changing adult incontinence items. The social model provides meals, activities, recreational programming, and health-related services. Social model adult day programs will use reminders or prompts to go to the toilet, take medicine, etc.

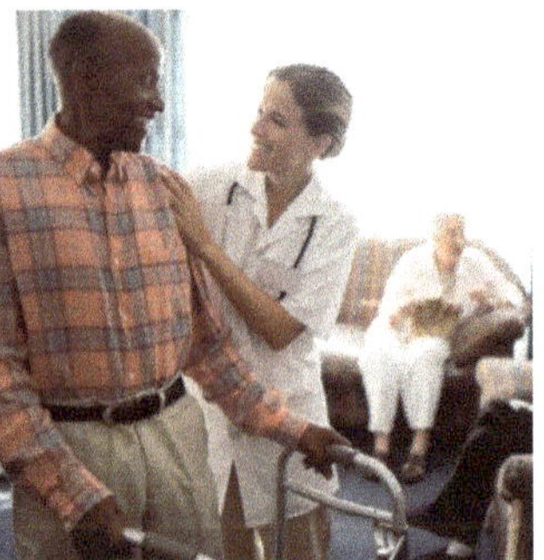

ASSISTED LIVING

Some long-term care insurance policies may cover assisted living costs. Assisted living communities help with Activities of Daily Living. Assisted living communities provide 24-hour on-site staffing, a resident nurse/on-site clinic, housekeeping, maintenance, laundry, recreational programs, exercise and wellness programs, nutritional meals and on-site dining, and transportation to and from medical appointments. Some assisted living communities serve disease-specific individuals such as those with Alzheimer's Disease and other dementias. Assisted living community care is for seniors who are in good health and want to maintain independence. Assisted living is appropriate for residents needing assistance with cooking, cleaning, and some personal upkeep. Assisted living communities are for help with bathing, using the toilet, and managing meds. The person needs to be active. Residents are usually not incontinent, can transfer independently and safely with a wheelchair without staff assistance or supervision, are not at risk for falls, and can eat independently.

COMPANION SERVICES

Usually, the programs involve non-medical care providers. They are generally privately paid for versus insurance paying for the program; although I have heard some long-term care insurance companies may cover the cost. The companions do not provide physical care such as bathing or dressing. They can prepare meals, do light housekeeping, and provide a reminder to take medications but are not to administer medication. Some companion agencies transport clients to medical appointments and run errands. Services vary by agency and by state regulations.

CONTINUING CARE COMMUNITIES

These community options vary by state. Some states offer senior houses, senior apartments, outpatient rehabilitation centers (physical, occupational, and speech therapy services), assisted living, and nursing home care. Some communities require a membership fee but will guarantee a person will remain in their community. I have worked in some faith-based communities, such as Jewish senior communities and the Masonic homes (Masons), which utilize this model of care.

HOME-DELIVERED MEALS

Some programs are run by towns and counties or via client insurance benefits. In my area of New York, some Medicaid managed care programs have contracts with meal delivery companies. Another option is meal delivery services such as Blue Apron, Factor, Hello Fresh, etc. I do not explicitly endorse any meal delivery programs. I recommend searching online for meal delivery programs for your region.

HOME HEALTH CARE

This includes private individuals or agencies who have certified nursing aides, personal care aides, and other medically trained personnel who provide care in the home. They offer light housekeeping of a loved one's space, physical care for Activities of Daily Living (ADLs) such as bathing and dressing, meal preparation, and medication administration, and may provide transportation services. Due to nationwide aide shortages, agencies have hired family members to care for a loved one in some states. Aides are usually privately paid for unless the person has a short-term rehabilitation need or is on Medicaid (state aid program).

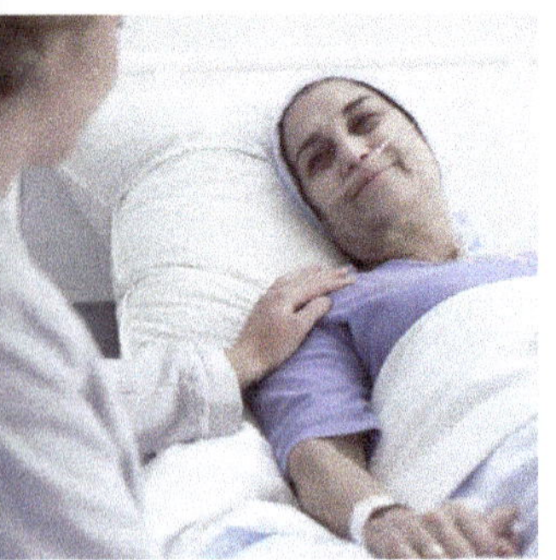

HOSPICE

Is a program for those at the end of life. Hospice is for those living with a serious illness. Hospice assists with pain relief, management of symptoms, and support of the individual and their family. Care can be provided in the home, and some regions have hospice care homes where an individual is admitted to a home staffing, high levels of nursing care, and supervision. Hospice care is billable under Medicare and other insurance plans (contact your local palliative care or hospice to review insurance coverage options). Starting hospice sooner rather than later is recommended. Hospice has a team of physicians, nurses, social workers, chaplains, volunteers, and other professionals as needed.

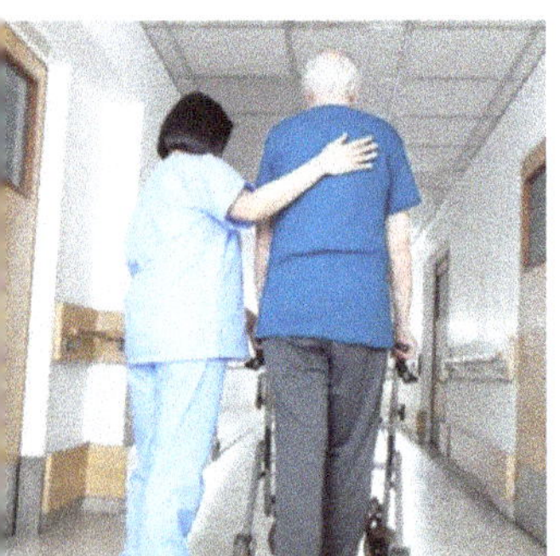

NURSING HOME (Skilled Nursing Facility)

Provides short-term rehabilitation and long-term care. Some long-term care policies may cover the cost of care, families may pay privately, or insurance may cover short-term rehabilitation. Insurance or Medicare covers the cost of short-term rehabilitation **IF** the person is progressing. Nursing homes provide 24-hour staffing and high levels of medical care. Nursing homes are for seniors with serious medical issues and chronic health needs. The care provided is hospital-level care. Nursing homes are ideal for limited mobility, chronic illness, inability to eat independently, incontinence, those with a risk of falling if not supervised, and a person who cannot transfer from a bed to a wheelchair without assistance.

PET CARETAKER

I have had families hire pet caretakers via Care.com or other online sites (NextDoor, Facebook, local ads). Sometimes, a friend or neighbor can assist a loved one with caring for a pet. A responsible teen or college student is also an option. For someone who is lonely and has no pets, some shelters help seniors by providing senior pets in the home and taking care of the pet's needs while allowing a loved one the companionship of an animal. The animals are usually older, unadoptable due to age or a medical condition, and are part of a program to meet the needs of a person and the animal.

SENIOR HOUSING, APARTMENTS, OR HOMES

Provide handicap-accessible living, may provide staff to administer medication, can be part of a group home environment where multiple people live in communal spaces, can be disease-specific, and some states have low-cost options for seniors who meet the income guidelines. I have not heard of them being covered by insurance companies, and I hope this changes as our aging population grows. There are state-specific guidelines for these homes.

ADDITIONAL INFORMATION

Some Long-term Care Insurance Plans may offer payment for home care, home-delivered meals (in my area, we have Mom's Meals and Meals on Wheels), assisted living, nursing home care, and other care options. Medicaid Managed Care companies (state-funded programs) may also offer meal delivery options.

Home health care can be combined with adult day programs. I have worked with seniors who had an aide get them ready in the morning, and they were then transported to an adult day program. Some adult day programs provide transportation. There also may be county or state transportation options to assist working families with getting a loved one to a program. I once worked for a company that provided transportation to an outpatient day program as part of their services.

Senior apartments may allow companion services, such as a non-medical care provider who assists with medication reminders, prepares meals, or sits with a loved one.

> Word of mouth is gold in trying to find assistance. I recommend family members reach out to people they know and be open to asking questions about referral options. I have obtained referrals from my hairdresser as she knows a lot of home health aides.

CHAPTER FIVE 

CAREGIVER PHYSICAL NEEDS AND THE IMPORTANCE OF SELF-CARE

As a social worker, I have heard the term caregiver selfishness, which is a trigger statement for me. I have listened to family members use this to criticize a caregiver who placed a loved one in respite care or a nursing home. Caregivers are not selfish in seeking assistance for their loved ones and themselves. Caregivers often neglect their health. This is one of my biggest concerns when I meet with a caregiver.

An example is when I ask a caregiver when their loved one's last appointment was, and caregivers can give me a list of recent appointments for their loved one. They will tell me the most recent date of bloodwork, cardiologist visit, primary care visit, dentist, etc. They can also tell me about any upcoming appointments.

When I ask the caregiver when their last appointment was, they have to stop and think about it or cannot remember. I often ask when the caregiver last went to the dentist, primary care physician, specialist, etc. I am often met with a long pause, sometimes a nervous laugh, a drop in eye contact as they glance at the floor, and a response of not remembering.

Caregivers may experience burnout from the stress of caring for someone else.

I tell caregivers they need to continue to care for themselves to provide care for their loved ones. I talk to them about preventative work versus crisis work and how my fear, as a social worker, is the caregiver having a crisis that impacts the person being cared for.

CAREGIVER CRISIS PREVENTION

This has been one of my most vital work areas as a social worker. A caregiver is hospitalized or passes away, or a caregiver is no longer able to take care of their loved one due to their own health crisis. I have seen many scenarios of this in many environments I have worked in, including my work with the Alzheimer's Association, assisted living, nursing homes, and dialysis clinics. I have seen caregivers pass away after neglecting their health, something unexpected happening, a tragedy like a caregiver who died in a car accident, and now there is a crisis. This is another way we can assist as social workers.

We can ask:
- Who will care for a loved one?
- How will care be provided?
- Who will take care of any pets?

When I work with caregivers, I emphasize having a crisis plan. I discuss my concerns or a dynamic I am seeing and identify potential risks to create a crisis prevention plan. I will ask to meet with the family, friends, church members, or any other support to create a crisis plan. After the meeting, I type up the plan and provide copies. I use an airplane oxygen analogy or tell them I am wearing a parachute if I jump out of a plane. A backup plan is a good idea and a written plan shared with others is helpful. I also emphasize how taking care of oneself is a benefit in assisting in caring for a loved one.

SERVICES

I recommend weighing the emotional impact on all involved, as it can be challenging to ask for help or to know what to ask for. Social workers and other healthcare professionals are often treasure hunters as we seek services. They often hear of programs, agencies, or services others offer. They can identify who provides what type of service and can combine service options. I will call Agency B and then Agency G to combine them to assist, as maybe one
includes transportation to a program for the other. Social workers and other healthcare professionals are seekers of services. They are the source for clients and others to go to when they are beginning to look into service options, are overwhelmed, or during a crisis.

Here are a few helpful tips.
- Can the loved one leave home?
    - I worked with a client with Alzheimer's who was terrified of leaving home as he lived by an airport. He believed he was still in the military. He had severe Post

Traumatic Stress Disorder (PTSD) and relived his war days each time he heard or saw a plane overhead. He lived near an Air Force base. He refused to leave the house, had boarded his windows, and would become violent when his wife tried to leave the home or coax him to leave the home. His wife would try to figure out the flight schedule. She would put a headset on him with music he enjoyed, minimizing the noise as she took him outside to get him to doctor's appointments.

- At times, there is a nagging or a lingering thought that services are needed, and at other times, there is a defining moment where in-home or out-of-home services are needed. The moment differs based on the individual.
  - For someone with Alzheimer's, it may be when the person is sundowning (confusing days and nights), wandering, or has behaviors.
  - For a person with Multiple Sclerosis, physical changes may require home care services such as an aide for bathing, transferring from a bed to a wheel-chair, and dressing.

- Does the caregiver have health issues requiring assistance and cannot continue in the role they had?

- What is the crisis plan?

PERCEPTIONS

Some of the common perceptions I have heard from my caregivers are:
- Feel pressure to balance it all.
- Has difficulty discussing the need for assistance (can be seen as a weakness or feeling guilty at being unable to provide care). I have experienced this with male and female care-givers who said, "I should be the one providing care for mom, dad, my partner, my spouse."
- Has to justify choices to family members, friends, co-workers, etc. During COVID, I saw this flare often. I worked with caregivers who had loved ones go into the hospital. At the beginning of COVID-19, no visitors were allowed in the hospital.
  - One client I worked with had co-workers judging her about her choices. They were saying, "Why aren't you going to visit your husband? You know the staff is busy, and he's being left alone. How do you know the hospital is taking care of him?... What are you doing just sitting around waiting for news?... You should go to the hospital and demand to see him." She was also told, "If I were you, I would buy scrubs and storm the hospital acting like a staff member." The client was very stressed about her husband and did not expect her work environment to add to her stress, worry, and anxiety about her husband's health.

As social workers and other healthcare professionals can counteract these perceptions and offer support. They can assist with boundary setting, support the choices the person is making, encourage support groups or reach out to other caregivers either in-person or online, and provide resource lists and articles or websites to educate our clients. I have dealt with family members who try to block other family members from assisting.

• They feel they must take it all on themselves. At other times, this is due to sibling dynamics. They do not want others involved. I have tried to work with family members and their loved ones, and I suggested a niece or nephew or someone connected to the sibling who the sibling will listen to. Is there a family friend who can try to assist with bridging? I also consider what the reason is that the person is blocking out other family members. What is the emotion behind it? I try different angles to solve this problem.

COMMON EMOTIONS CAREGIVERS HAVE TOLD ME THEY EXPERIENCE

- ◆ Anger
- ◆ Anxiety
- ◆ Denial
- ◆ Depression
- ◆ Doubt/second-guessing
- ◆ Grief/Loss
- ◆ Guilt
- ◆ Shame
- ◆ Shame

SECOND GUESSING

This is a natural part of caregiving. This is where the coulda, woulda, shoulda comes in. There will be emotional ups and downs, such as feelings of grief related to a loved one who was placed in a nursing home (long-term care facility).

Memory can fade, and we can often view things more positively than they were at the time. There may be a caregiver who, once they have an aide, believes they provided better care than the aide. When someone is placed in a long-term care facility, they are critical of the care the staff provides. "I was providing better care than they are."
- • Often, this comes up as the caregiver has reduced stress, improved sleep, and less worry about a loved one's day-to-day needs.
- • Recalling events like "Mom only hit a fence leaving the diner. No one was injured. Maybe she could have driven longer, or we could have let her drive locally. Maybe we did not need to take the car keys."

There will be the question of whether the right decision was made. Caregivers need to be reminded that they are making the best decisions for themselves and their loved ones.

I have run into this challenge when there are instances of cognitive impairment, and the person cannot make decisions for themselves or about their care options due to Alzheimer's Disease, a stroke, or a coma. I will walk the family members through a visualization exercise where I will ask them to visualize their loved one standing next to them as an observer.
I will ask the person, "If Dad could stand next to you and see himself as he is right now, what would he want you to do? What would he tell you to do?" I will say, "ask (Mom, Dad, or say the person's name) to consider… (the options being presented)." It could be they ask:

Would Mom want to be tube-fed?

Would Dad want to be intubated (*have his airway opened with a tube to breathe*) or put on life support?

Would they want me to put them on dialysis?

Would they want to live like they are right now?

Would they want me to keep them comfortable and let them pass away?

Would they consider their current situation as quality of life?

What was important to them?
- The ability to spend time with family?
- To go fishing?
- The ability to eat on their own?
- The ability to breathe on their own?
- The ability to make decisions or think?

I cannot tell you how often family members become emotional during this exercise or siblings stop arguing about what to do. This is also a useful tool with a person who will not let anyone assist or block others. I will ask them who Mom or Dad would want to help. Often, this exercise helps the person separate from the emotion and reduces second-guessing.

EMOTIONS

Some caregivers and loved ones may feel violated with in-home services. This was my father when my grandmother moved in with my parents. He wanted to pick the hours of care. Sometimes, there is a transition as the person being cared for may feel vulnerable with someone bathing, dressing, or toileting them. There is vulnerability in needing someone to assist you.

The loved one is feeling vulnerability:
- For themselves.
- For their loved one.
- For their family's privacy as service providers enter the home.

Consider:
- Providers will have a schedule as determined by their agency or the available hours, which may differ from the schedule a family wants.
- The daily routines of the home will change. The structure of the family unit will change how the family members manage their roles.
- Care providers will do a job as their agency or state regulations outline. A caregiver may expect an aide to clean the whole home. Often the agency will clean shared spaces the loved one uses, such as a bedroom, bathroom, and kitchen area; not the entire house.

Emotions can vary.
- Frequency, intensity, duration, and type of emotions.
- Emotions are individualized and need to be considered.

CHAPTER SIX

RESPITE

Respite care is a service that can be used ito provide short term relief for caregivers in their home or outside of the home. I have worked with caregivers who used respite to have time alone at home, recuperate from their own illness or surgery, take a vacation, or attend a special event such as a wedding a loved one could not attend.

Here is some information about respite care:
- Respite helps prevent caregiver burnout.
- I worked in an assisted living community, and a woman was admitted for a weekend. She said to her daughter, "I am going to be dead by the time you get back. I hope you enjoy your vacation. I can't believe you did this to me." She guilted the daughter. The daughter left sobbing, and I walked her to her car and told her to give her Mom a few hours, and I would call the daughter with an update on how Mom was doing. The daughter left. An hour later, I went to check on Mom, and I am not kidding when I say Mom opened the door as soon as I knocked, peeked out, and here is our conversation.

> Mom: "Is my daughter gone?"
>
> Me: "Yes."
>
> Mom: "Oh good. I heard the chef here is phenomenal, and I am going to the dining room to meet up with a friend who lives here."
>
> Mom then wheeled past me in her wheelchair to enter the dining room. I almost burst out laughing as I had just witnessed the dynamic of the mother with her daughter, and the Mom was okay. I did call the daughter to tell her that her mother was fine and was eating in the dining hall.

- There are respite care costs, which are usually not covered by insurance. It is worth checking with your insurance company to confirm if respite care is an option. Some long-term care plans may cover the cost of respite.
- Prices vary by region.
- Local area agencies would have more information on regionally specific resources.

- I also encourage using relatives, friends, neighbors, and church members as options for respite care. Often, unpaid caregivers can assist.
- During COVID, I worked in a dialysis clinic, and transportation companies were unwilling to bring patients to the clinic due to fear of staff catching COVID. We could not get patients to their treatment, and without treatment, the person can die. It was a catch-22 situation. We had to network with relatives, friends, neighbors, and other dialysis patients who were driving themselves to treatment and move patient schedules to assist with carpooling options and church members.

Look at other opportunities in informal networks that are not formal agencies.

I am a big fan of respite care.

FINANCIAL ASPECTS OF CAREGIVING

The services outlined in this presentation can vary in cost, from private payments to state aid insurance such as Medicaid.

Rates can vary based on the services by state and the level of services needed.

Private pay is straightforward, as services are paid for out-of-pocket.

Grants – although rare – can be used. COVID significantly impacted grants, and agencies modified their programs to accommodate the need. Some agencies tightened grant eligibility requirements.
  - A tip about grants - some are for one-time usage, and some can be reapplied annually.

Medicaid/state income-based insurance - I found the following website helpful in identifying Medicaid programs by state https://www.medicaid.gov/state-overviews/index.html.
- Income eligibility must be met.
- Criteria for eligibility vary by state.
- Types of coverage vary – HMO and community resource coverage options vary.
- There are also severe nursing aide shortages nationwide, and some agencies may pay family members, friends, and neighbors to care for loved ones. The aides can pick the cases they want and be more selective than in the past due to the shortages.

Veterans and the VA System – I have successfully referred caregivers to the local VA for assistance. Some VA centers have assisted living and nursing home care. I had a daughter of a patient on dialysis whom the VA paid to be his caregiver. In my region, I had to refer to the VA, which is an hour and a half away. Satellite offices are often impacted by funding and staff shortages. I have contacted county VA advocates who are not VA employees and serve to assist veterans in the county. They try to bridge services with the VA for veterans.

What is the Difference Between Medicare and Medicaid (state aid programs)?

The Terms Medicare And Medicaid can be confusing
- MEDICARE is a federal program covering short-term services such as hospitalization and skilled rehabilitation centers. It will not pay for 24-hour care in the home or for permanent nursing home care.

  - In the dialysis world, it does cover dialysis long-term with some limitations to coverage (covers 80% of care/**NOT** 100%). Check eligibility guidelines and talk to your dialysis social worker, as there are exceptions to Medicare eligibility.

- MEDICAID is a state-run program that covers some long-term services such as home health aide if income and health criteria are met. Medicaid also covers long-term care, such as skilled nursing facilities (nursing homes). Medicaid can also be used as a secondary insurance in conjunction with Medicare. Guidelines and income criteria vary by state.

SUPPORT SYSTEMS

◆ Church ◆ Community agencies ◆ Family
◆ Friends ◆ Support groups ◆ Volunteer agencies

Emotional, physical, and financial support are all needed when caregiving.

Some states, counties, and localities have a warm check-in where volunteers call to check in on home-bound elderly. They are a lifeline for emotional support and are usually affiliated with agencies. Some disease-specific organizations offer 24-hour caregiver assistance where volunteers or social workers manage phone lines.

Social workers and other healthcare professions can assist with encouraging clients to ask for help.

They are instrumental in identifying community resources.

CHAPTER SEVEN 

HOW SOCIAL WORKERS AND OTHER HEALTHCARE PROFESSIONALS CAN HELP

Social Workers and Healthcare Professionals are essential to caregivers. I cannot emphasize this enough.

Social Workers and Healthcare Professionals look at the whole person and the systems impacting the caregiver and their loved one. They look at how "this plus this" affects a caregiver and their loved one. They can see system strengths and system limits.

They are skilled in identifying resources and service gaps. Where are the service gaps, and how do we fill these gaps?

They are knowledgeable about our communities.

Social Workers and Healthcare Professionals are navigators of systems, such as understanding insurance programs and completing applications (for transportation/home-delivered meals/grants).

Social Workers and Healthcare Professionals can offer counseling and refer to or facilitate support groups.

They are masters at networking.

> When I worked in dialysis, I bordered several counties, and all day long, I wore my case management hat. Sometimes, I wanted to pull my hair out. Geographically, the dialysis clinic was the nearest clinic to a patient, but because of county transportation boundaries, I could not get my patients to the dialysis clinic. The patient would have to go to a clinic 30 minutes away in his/her county versus mine, within 5 to 10 minutes of their home. The neighboring county van would drive three exits past my dialysis clinic to drop off patients at a mall, but we could not add a stop half a mile off the exit to get patients to dialysis. My patients could be picked up at the mall by the county I was in, take three buses, and be brought to my dialysis clinic. I spent hours on the phone with both county transportation departments to make them aware of how this impacted the dialysis patients' health. I tried to get them to coordinate and meet with me to address how to make this system more user-friendly.

CONCLUSION

This book and the presentation it was based on discusses caregiving through various aspects, including perception, roles, levels of care, and financial resources. I hope you have found this information useful as you help individuals and families navigate the complexities of caregiving.

Local area agencies such as Offices for the Aging and the Department of Social Services can assist.

www.aarp.org

American Association of Retired Persons – can choose topics from legal, health, family, etc.

www.caregiver.com

is a source for caregivers, including a magazine, newsletter, and resources.

www.caregiving.org

National Alliance for Caregiving – a non-profit coalition of national organizations to support family caregivers. The coalition provides research, advocates, raises public awareness and looks at policies impacting family caregivers.

https://eldercare.acl.gov/Public/lndex.aspx

Department of Health and Human Services
- Search local service organizations in your community
- Search the Aging Network
- Resources

www.hhs.gov

U.S. Department of Health and Human Services – choose a topic to search

https://www.medicaid.gov/state-overviews/index.html

American Association of Retired Persons – can choose topics from legal, health, family, etc.

SUPPORT GROUPS

- Disease-specific groups
- Caregiver groups – live or online

REFERENCE

National Academies of Sciences, Engineering, and Medicine (2016). Families caring for an aging America. The National Academies Press. https://doi.org/10.17226/23606.

Notes

Notes